It's Challah Time!

KAR-BEN PUBLISHING®
An imprint of Lerner Publishing Group, Inc.
241 First Avenue North
Minneapolis, MN 55401 USA

Website address: www.karben.com

Main body text set in Futura Std Medium.
Typeface provided by Adobe Systems.

Library of Congress Cataloging-in-Publication Data

Names: Kropf, Latifa Berry, author.
Title: It's challah time! / Latifa Berry Kropf.
Description: Minneapolis : Kar-Ben Publishing , [2020] | Series: Shabbat | 20th
    anniversary edition. | Audience: Ages 2–6 | Audience: Grades K–1 | Summary:
    "In this 20th anniversary edition of Kar-Ben's best-seller with all new photos, a
    diverse preschool class demonstrates the steps of making challah—the special
    braided bread eaten on Shabbat"— Provided by publisher.
Identifiers: LCCN 2019042995 (print) | LCCN 2019042996 (ebook) | ISBN
    9781541574601 (paperback) | ISBN 9781541599581 (ebook)
Subjects: LCSH: Challah (Bread)—Juvenile literature.
Classification: LCC BM657.C43 K76 2020 (print) | LCC BM657.C43 (ebook) |
    DDC 641.5/67641—dc23

LC record available at https://lccn.loc.gov/2019042995
LC ebook record available at https://lccn.loc.gov/2019042996

PJ Library Edition ISBN 978-1-5415-7461-8

Manufactured in China
1-46594-47601-12/11/2019

062031.2K4/B176/A3

It's
Challah
Time!

Latifa Berry Kropf

photography by **Moshe Shai**

KAR-BEN
PUBLISHING

Hooray, it's Friday!
We are going to bake challah for Shabbat!

How do we make challah?
Shayla pours flour into a large bowl.

Benjy adds yeast, so the dough will rise.

Orly adds honey to the bowl
to make the challah sweet and delicious.

Mira pours in the oil.
Careful, not too much!

What's next? Right! Eggs!

All the ingredients are in the bowl.
Now we mix and mix and mix.
The dough is very sticky!

We have to knead and knead the dough until it's smooth.
It's hard work!

While the dough rests, it rises.
It's so hard to be patient.
When will the dough be ready?

Look how much it's grown!
Our dough is ready.

Now it's time to prepare the challahs.
We divide the dough into three strips and braid them together.

The challahs are big, beautiful, and ready to bake.
Mira brushes them with egg.
It's like painting with watercolors!

We wave good-bye to the challahs.
Our teacher, Anna, will carry them to the oven.

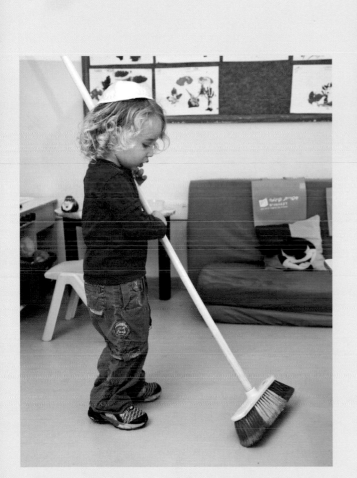

While we wait for the challahs to bake,
we tidy up the room for Shabbat.
Our Shabbat celebration will be joyful.

Look! The challahs are ready!

The table is set.
Anna lights the candles and we say the blessings.

We drink grape juice.
The taste of Shabbat is sweet.

We reach for the warm challahs and say the special blessing.

Finally, it's time to taste our challahs. They are so delicious!
Shabbat Shalom!

Whole Wheat Honey Challah

2 Tbsp. yeast
½ cup warm water
1 tsp. honey

4 cups whole wheat flour
½ cup oil
½ cup honey (less the teaspoon mixed with the yeast)

2 eggs
2 tsp. salt
1 Tbsp. cinnamon
1 Tbsp. vanilla
1½ cups warm water

Up to 3 cups white flour
Poppy seeds, sesame seeds, or cinnamon/sugar mixture for top

In a small bowl, mix yeast with ½ cup warm water, and a bit of the honey. Let it bubble.

In a large bowl, mix the wheat flour, oil, eggs, salt, cinnamon, vanilla, and the rest of the honey. Add the yeast mixture and 1½ cups warm water. Add the white flour one cup at a time and when the dough is firm, begin kneading it. Add more white flour as needed. The dough should not be sticky.

Put the dough in an oiled bowl and cover it with a damp cloth. Let it rise for one hour.

Punch down the dough to remove the air bubbles. Form loaves. This recipe makes four large loaves.

Place the loaves on cookie sheets that have been oiled or covered with parchment. Sprinkle with a topping of your choice.

Bake in a preheated oven at 325 degrees for 20 minutes. Place on a rack to cool . . . and enjoy!

Blessings

Over the candles

בָּרוּךְ אַתָּה יְיָ אֱלֹהֵינוּ מֶלֶךְ הָעוֹלָם,
אֲשֶׁר קִדְּשָׁנוּ בְּמִצְוֹתָיו וְצִוָּנוּ לְהַדְלִיק נֵר שֶׁל שַׁבָּת.

Baruch Atah Adonai Eloheinu Melech ha'olam,
asher kid'shanu b'mitzvotav v'tzivanu l'hadlik ner shel Shabbat.

Blessed are You, our God, Ruler of the world, who has made us holy
and has given us the mitzvah of lighting the Shabbat candles.

Over the grape juice/wine

בָּרוּךְ אַתָּה יְיָ אֱלֹהֵינוּ מֶלֶךְ הָעוֹלָם, בּוֹרֵא פְּרִי הַגָּפֶן.

Baruch Atah Adonai Eloheinu Melech ha'olam, borei p'ri hagafen.

Blessed are You, our God, Ruler of the world,
who has created the fruit of the vine.

Over the challah

בָּרוּךְ אַתָּה יְיָ אֱלֹהֵינוּ מֶלֶךְ הָעוֹלָם, הַמּוֹצִיא לֶחֶם מִן הָאָרֶץ.

Baruch Atah Adonai Eloheinu Melech ha'olam, hamotzi lechem min ha'aretz.

Blessed are You, our God, Ruler of the world,
who gives us bread from the earth.